Things That MATTER

DR. WILBUR HILL

ISBN 978-1-0980-6046-6 (paperback)
ISBN 978-1-0980-6047-3 (digital)

Christian Faith Publishing, Inc.
832 Park Avenue
Meadville, PA 16335
www.christianfaithpublishing.com

Printed in the United States of America

I can do all things through him
who strengthens me.
(Philippians 4:13)

This book is dedicated to Amos Jr., Gladys, Sherleon, Alvin and Wellington. Thank you for your years of support and encouragement.

CONTENTS

PART ONE

Tips on Caring and Growing in Life

LIFE **IS** LIKE

riding a bicycle

TO KEEP YOUR

BALANCE

you must keep moving

thinking
emotion optimist mind
communication opportunity fit
ecstatic concentration potential idea
idealistic intelligence brainstorm improve
confident teamwork thought success mindset health
think positive
inspiration creativity attitude attractive wisdom
competitive psychology concept smile
leadership health happy inspire
winner strenght emotional
wisdom bright
smart

CHAPTER 1

Leaning on Learning, Productivity, and Positive Thinking

You can make your tomorrow by starting it today; but once tomorrow comes the precious opportunity to seize control of it has already passed you by.

* * * * *

Thinking positive produces the same outcome every time.

* * * * *

What we learn is to be shared. That is your reasonable learned contribution to society.

* * * * *

A dream will always be a dream until you drag it with an action into reality.

* * * * *

What you think can be changed, and what you change makes all the difference.

* * * * *

What you did today should have been aimed at a better tomorrow. If it was not, you just missed another day to make life and living better for you or someone else.

* * * * *

Stay away from wasted time as it is addictive and stealthily fosters a wasted life, in time. It is close to being dead; immobile and doing nothing.

* * * * *

Learn to laugh. It is a self-generated medi-cation that makes your insides feel much better.

* * * * *

Running away from life's challenges is a sur-render to victory. It is likely not the victory you would be proud of and hope for though.

* * * * *

Stand to fight—rise above depression; think positive impressions.

* * * * *

Live well today because that will facilitate your tomorrow for better or you will end up with worst.

* * * * *

If you have no peace you have no meaning-ful position in life. If you have no position, you have no purpose. If you have no purpose, you have nothing of benefit to offer for yourself or anyone else. Do not give into a dead life. Find your position of purpose for benefit.

* * * * *

Vacations are important. They let you vacate the stress of living and refresh you for new begin-nings. Everyone needs them or you will always be stuck in the same creature-of-habit rut.

* * * * *

Everyone should have an established goal to help someone by some means during the course of a year. Doing so helps you not to forget to do so by year's end.

* * * * *

If you have no goals in life you will not feel compelled to achieve anything. Do not be another leaf in the wind not knowing when or where it will land. Define your destiny today.

* * * * *

Education is a good thing until you think you are better than others. Then your education becomes meaningless and you become a member of the unintelligent society having not truly learned from the things you supposedly learned.

* * * * *

Taking responsibility for your actions is not always an easy thing to do, but it truly brands the content of your character for others.

* * * * *

Every successful person will have discouragement and perseverance in their showdown box of experiences.

* * * * *

Being successful will have much to do with fostering the success for those around you.

* * * * *

A camp of successful people will reproduce the same. A camp of losers will produce the same ongoing reproductions and there is therefore no need to second guess it. Who are you hanging around with now?

* * * * *

How far has God brought you? Recount every personal occasion you may have been at risk and could have fallen gravely ill or died. It will help to grow your gratification by recounting your blessings.

* * * * *

Perfection is built slowly because the essence of its strength is laced in attention to details.

* * * * *

A long hard road to success is the only sure gateway to a prosperous life of rest.

* * * * *

Your loss of status or valuables will be unfortunate, but that will never measure up to the loss of your soul. Until any thief can rob you of our soul, you really have not lost much at all.

* * * * *

It will always be more meaningful and profitable to run any race to the finish line than to win. Achievement for all is at the end of the line. Winning has to do with status and only one will claim it. But everyone can claim achievement if they cross the finish line, which is why we set out to do anything. Winning is nice, but achievement is a momentous benchmark in our lives.

* * * * *

When you focus on the negative, you negate all sorts of untapped potential and opportunities that would have otherwise been yours had you not been processing in negative context. Stay positive.

* * * * *

Help is always one prayer away.

* * * * *

Look for ways to do what everyone else is doing—better. You could become the next self-made millionaire.

* * * * *

An unproductive minute is a deductive minute from an improved quality of life for you or someone around you.

* * * * *

Walking away from God, I do not dare; waiting until the moment when I am caught up in the air.

* * * * *

The sooner you start, the sooner your dream is realized.

* * * * *

It is simple—you can be a standout by taking meaningful actions to stand-out. Figure it out.

* * * * *

You can discover much more about yourself by being quiet and looking inward. We often do not take time to do it though. Many people have come to know us by observation more than we have come to know ourselves. Look inside yourself to see what they see.

* * * * *

Nothing worth having is without sacrifice or it is otherwise worthless.

* * * * *

The healing power of laughter is a free emotion medication with no co-pays.

* * * * *

Preoccupation in busy activities serves as a great stress and anxiety buster.

* * * * *

A mistake made once is understandable, but the same mistake twice draws into question your ability to learn.

* * * * *

If you run from achievement, you are always one more step away from success with every step you take.

* * * * *

If you do not rise to points of exhaustion in the things you do, you are not doing them well enough.

* * * * *

Don't ask where's mine…go get it!

* * * * *

If you have vision, you can see God's creations. If you have hands, you can feel them. God is all around us.

* * * * *

Not knowing what to do is the notice for you to do something. Something always makes a difference. Finding something is your new job to knowing something. Once you realize something, you then know what to do. So, do something.

* * * * *

Rocky starts do not necessarily mean you will have a rocky end, unless you failed to move the rock.

* * * * *

Perseverance precedes success.

* * * * *

You will always have opportunity and opposition. How you respond to either will define you and your future.

* * * * *

All prevailing good things came from good people.

* * * * *

Rich in money is good, but rich in character is lifelong wealth.

* * * * *

Your heart and actions are one and the same.

* * * * *

Insurance is a funny thing. We really do not want it but cannot afford to not have it. We always need to pay it, but you never really want a cause to use it.

* * * * *

The accolade of success is cloaked in your determination.

* * * * *

Successful people have many stories to tell and most often many of them will be instances of failure.

* * * * *

Suffering makes you appreciate the good times and further reminds us of when it was not a present state of life.

* * * * *

Quality of life starts with your insistence of having one.

* * * * *

When you conclude you're no better than the person who cleans toilets for a living, you will have humbly come to respect God's plan and assignment for every precious person—no matter who they are or what they do.

* * * * *

Doing your best is all anyone can reasonably expect of you. If they expect more, they need to pick another person.

* * * * *

Immorality is a tempting and dangerous enemy who has stolen and destroyed countless families and careers. It laughs at us because it sees how we continue to entertain its company without resistance to stop the cycle of insanity. Have your efforts to stop failed? If yes, take it to God for him to confront the enemy on your behalf. You just won this battle!

* * * * *

The road to success is long, but so is the road to peace and relaxation following success.

* * * * *

A walk on the wide side is not necessarily dangerous unless you are walking through the wild.

*　*　*　*　*

The best fish are in the deep waters or anything else worthwhile for that matter. Always go deep for the best of the best.

*　*　*　*　*

The best people to surround yourself with will be those who are the best at what they do.

*　*　*　*　*

Be first at something. Set a goal to be the first to accomplish something. The opportunities are many and all around you. Just look for them. Be the first woman, man, minority to... I was the first categorical minority to hold two different executive positions in my career. Go ahead and make a statement for yourself and the group you most closely represent.

*　*　*　*　*

Waiting for the right timing on something is hard, but not as hard as the loss and regret connected to the wrong timing.

* * * * *

Pain and suffering quickly brings into focus the retrospective of times that we were not in that state.

* * * * *

Suffering in any context or measure is undesirable but learning from it is an invaluable commodity for future reference.

* * * * *

Education is one of the best gateways to success.

* * * * *

A waste of time is theft from yourself and God.

* * * * *

Being strong is an intentional engagement of strength. Being strong is strength at work.

* * * * *

Strength in anything is the consistent exercise of the presence of energy.

* * * * *

Stability is balanced existence in motion.

* * * * *

Everyone should have a label that defines who they are and marks their brand without statement. Keep in mind that your demeanor and conduct normally takes care of that for you.

* * * * *

Isolation is the closest realization of death.

* * * * *

Everyone has an art capacity. What is yours to share?

* * * * *

Discover yourself with meditation.

* * * * *

What have you accomplished in the last five years? What does your next five years hold? If you do not know, your GPS may take you anywhere, even to undesirable destinations.

* * * * *

Moving in the right direction is always paramount or you otherwise end up in all the wrong places.

* * * * *

Vigilance is a virtue which precipitates increased awareness about the many opportunities around us.

* * * * *

Knowledge is the beginning and end of success.

* * * * *

Opposition is sometimes good. It makes us consider alternatives.

* * * * *

Fear can be crippling but increasing one's knowledge to overcome it evokes power.

* * * * *

How you see yourself is often played out in the display of your self-confidence.

* * * * *

Thinking about getting things done is useless, unless you move to get things done...one at a time.

* * * * *

Seeing things from different perspectives is brilliance on the way to success.

* * * * *

Home is where your heart is and where you end up. Be sure that your house is where you want to be. If not, change your heart.

* * * * *

The validation of friendship manifests itself with presence—in the good times and bad times.

* * * * *

Strength is applied energy at work in any cause.

* * * * *

Good relationships will fill many of your holes of inadequacy, so make sure you have reliable ones that you can count on when you need them most.

* * * * *

Pain can sometimes be defined as opportunity in disguise.

* * * * *

Performance vision is something everyone has access to, but innovative vision is something everyone rarely has access to.

* * * * *

Visionaries are always looking at things from untraditional perspectives. As a contextual example, you likely see the word "Start" here, but from the same word a visionary likely sees "Start tar tart star art sta." They see beyond what is in front of them. Whereas you see a word, they see the possibility of a complete sentence building upon the word.

* * * * *

If you cannot run, walk. If you cannot walk, crawl. If you cannot crawl, roll over. Whatever it takes, finish the race of challenge before you.

* * * * *

A true winner of any race is anyone who crosses the finish line. First place only verifies who finished first.

* * * * *

Anything worth having is something worth working toward.

* * * * *

Sacrifice and investment go together.

* * * * *

Building a successful life is much like building a house. The finished product will meet your expectation if you follow the blueprint. Otherwise, you may end up with a pile of junk. Make sure you develop or revalidate your life's blueprints to be sure you are building something you will be pleased with.

* * * * *

Those who wait on perfection can expect it in excellent fashion, but those who hasten to experience it will be short-changed and will miss out on its evolving and abundant offerings.

* * * * *

Give everyone the opportunity to disappoint you first.

* * * * *

You have two choices in life. You can let it happen or you can make it happen.

* * * * *

Unplanned success is generally short-lived, but planned success has long-lasting roots that will keep on giving back.

* * * * *

Sacrifice is always part of success with anything worthwhile.

* * * *

Your credibility is something you should always work to protect by being honest and forthcoming. It will serve you well when it is called into question by unfair context. On the other hand, if you lack credibility, you can hardly expect anyone to place confidence in your statements even if they are true.

* * * *

Time is precious and cannot be recovered. Make the best of it so you will not have a story to tell about how you became a loser. Of course, that will likely find its way into the category of untold stories.

* * * *

Words may not necessarily break your bones, but they can surely crush your spirit.

* * * * *

Ethical behavior is a reflection of the heart.

* * * * *

Production and determination are one and the same with anything we aspire to.

* * * * *

You cannot feel bad if you chose to feel good. The two cannot coexist.

* * * * *

Thought is good and bad. Which side you chose to be on makes all the difference in the quality of life you chose to live.

* * * * *

You are what you think. Positive thoughts foster more of the same and negative thoughts more of the same. You will always be in the company of one or the other. Choose discerningly smart by staying positive.

* * * * *

Military service is a conscious act of commitment to sacrificially die for what is perceptively right. A service member can give noting beyond their risk and exposure to death to ensure you retain peace, freedom and the quality of life you have come to know. Say thank you when you see one. They will appreciate the acknowledgement and that is the least we can do for them.

* * * * *

Have many friends, but always make sure you have only one best friend and a few reliable friends. Invest time with them. When the time gets tough, you will only find these friends in your company. All the other so-called friend imposters will be nowhere to be found.

* * * * *

Make a habit of committing to prayer before engaging any major undertaking or experience. It will make all the difference for your actions, response, and outcomes.

* * * * *

Realizing what you are weak at is a profound strength.

* * * * *

Do many things in life, but do at least one—very, very well.

* * * * *

If you think you will fail at something, you have already started to fail by moving forward without any actual evidence of failure itself.

* * * * *

Make your convictions about life and living and stand by them. You will otherwise be subject to being trampled.

* * * * *

Practice makes perfect—But if you practice it the wrong way, you will be "perfectly" wrong every time.

* * * * *

Success is not automatic; it is a manual process driven by determination.

* * * * *

If you have no goals in life, that within itself is a goal.

* * * * *

A successful marriage is not automatic, it is a manual process driven by determination.

* * * * *

Motivation is the realization that profitability exists in something we have been exposed to.

* * * * *

True quality time is the time spent improving the status of your life or someone else's.

* * * * *

A solid friendship helps to ground us and has interactive time as a testament of allegiance.

* * * * *

How much money is enough? To have money is to hope for money. There now, you have it—but it is not enough and never will be.

* * * * *

Tribulation is like snow; it lands, but must eventually dissipate.

* * * * *

Joy and happiness are both choices.

* * * * *

You have no story to tell if you have not lived one worth telling.

* * * * *

Do not be quick to reject constructive criticism. It invites us to think on and reassess our course of action and direction.

* * * * *

Happiness is not automatic; it is a manual process driven by determination.

* * * * *

Achievement is a commitment to accomplishing goals.

* * * * *

Peace begins when you step out of the chaos.

* * * * *

Make daily, weekly, monthly, and quarterly resolutions. The long-term yearly resolutions are less effective and hard to keep. Shorter resolutions work better because they will generally encourage you to get them done given that they are closest to you in time. You will also develop a sense of accomplishment and motivation to continue your journey by way of your small achievements. Long range plans are good if progressively managed, but they generally become pitfalls for procrastination and foster a lack of motivation and commitment for following through on them.

* * * * *

Life is the integration of our existence and experiences.

* * * * *

The quality of life is determined by the application of desired improvements into our experiences.

* * * * *

Destiny is a voluntary or involuntary direction of life. Destiny is as different to each one of us as our DNA and genetic influences. Destiny, however, has a capacity to be influenced. You have some choices here...make some good ones.

* * * * *

What plant can grow to its fullest potential with sunshine alone? It requires rain also. Our lives are similar, we experience the good, but the bad also has a role in helping us reach our maximum potential.

CHAPTER 2

Acts of Giving and Serving

To give is to get. What you get in return will generally be more than you could give.

* * * *

Giving produces reciprocal generosities. Unknown and unseen reciprocation is generally engaged by others when you need it most.

* * * *

Your willing service has no limits. Your benefit from service will likewise have no limits. People will instinctively want to serve you.

* * * *

What you have was given to you and therefore it was never yours to keep. What are you doing with yours?

* * * * *

If you do not give love and support, you can hardly expect to get it.

* * * * *

Give expecting nothing in return. Your return will likely become more than you could have ever given and at the most opportune time.

* * * * *

Always try to acknowledge the presence of others with a smile or hello. It confirms you are human, and they are too. Not even a robot or computer would acknowledge each other unless a human directed them to do so... so go ahead and act human. Make people feel good by acknowledging and recognizing them. It sometimes will be a surprise to them, but much appreciated.

* * * * *

Knowledge is meant to be shared. Anything short of that can be termed as selfish theft.

* * * * *

When you help someone; they never forget it. When you hurt someone; they never forget it. Which moment of recall do you prefer to be remembered by?

* * * * *

What have you done for someone else— lately?

* * * * *

A friend is there in the bad times when you need them and in the good times when you do not need them. Friendship's foundation is presence.

* * * * *

Service to others is generally a good alternative to replacing pain and suffering; theirs and yours.

* * * * *

If there is any respect to be had, it starts with your display of the same, even toward the most disrespectful of persons.

* * * * *

Your spouse or partner is waiting, without saying it, for you to make them feel good. What are you waiting on? They will reciprocate or learn to do so in time.

* * * * *

If you would like to feel good and accomplished—serve others.

* * * * *

If you cannot help—hopefully, you will pray.

* * * * *

It is impossible to help others without helping yourself, growing in love and character.

* * * * *

No act of kindness is ever lost in your mind and certainly not in the mind of the recipient.

* * * * *

Be true to yourself so it can reciprocate. It is an invisible medicine for the soul.

* * * * *

Your life experience was just that—yours. But others can benefit greatly from your achievements and shortcomings. We would all be a smarter people if you shared.

* * * * *

If you helped someone today, you help humanity progress.

* * * * *

As a rule, if you cannot help someone by your actions, keep your comments to yourself unless you are asked to share them.

* * * * *

Exercise fairness when engaging with others, so that you can reasonably expect reciprocal responses.

* * * * *

If you called on someone for help and they would not do it, do not fret, because that person was not the individual meant to help you. It is the person that ultimately will do so, so keep moving until you get the right person. That person will likely be able to help you well beyond what your needs demand.

* * * * *

You can improve your spirit and emotional well-being by helping others.

* * * * *

Kind acts will always be returned to you in abundance.

* * * * *

Company to the lonely is a priceless commodity you want to always say you offered.

* * * * *

A person in need is never far from you, so keep attuned to your opportunities to help around you.

* * * * *

Your gift, whatever it is, is never fully qualified as such until you share it.

* * * * *

A mentor is someone who does not mind sharing and the opposite of that is selfishness.

* * * * *

Surrender to service and service will serve you when you need it most.

* * * * *

If you have not helped your neighbor with anything lately, how is it that you will feel worthy of such support and assistance in your time of need?

* * * * *

Peace with oneself comes when we get busy with giving peace to others.

CHAPTER 3

Statements That Speak

What you say has less meaning if you did not mean what you said.

* * * * *

You can make a statement, or you can make a difference. Words or actions are defining moments that truly define you.

* * * * *

Your words should be kind and your heart ready to forgive. The opposite affect is harsh and unforgiving and that person should likewise be expecting the same and ready to confront.

* * * * *

Listen closely to what a person says and pay specific attention to what was left unsaid. That was the other part of the story you may have missed.

* * * * *

Quick judgment generally produces the same assessment about you from others because they see that is how you are and assume you wish them to do the same for you. If that is not how you intend others to see you, quickly fix this judgmental brand.

* * * * *

What you said has more to do with what was meant. Intent is always discerningly parked at the heart of any statement.

* * * * *

Your words can break a heart or spirit. Use them wisely.

* * * * *

Be quite and let the broken-hearted speak. That sensitive courtesy will stand to medicate the broken because they are able to safely talk about a brokenness in your presence of caring. It carries a lot of positive and uplifting mileage for the broken.

* * * * *

A rush to judgment says more about you than what you had to say.

* * * * *

Talk followed by action is serious business—no matter the subject.

* * * * *

Harsh responses cut away at your credibility and foster disrespect.

* * * * *

Flying off the handle may get you hit with a handle so handle yourself accordingly.

* * * * *

Gossip is ugly and so is your character if you give yourself permission to engage in the nonsense.

* * * * *

Truth can always stand to be repeated with accuracy, but a lie will always need help to survive. Lies are always sealed with the need to expound upon, justify, or further embellish it to help with its believability. The birth of one lie generally manifests itself into a cyclone of unmanageable and ongoing inaccuracies.

* * * * *

A lie is an addictive act that stealthily stages a commitment of repetition. Stop now to kill the cycle of insanity.

* * * * *

Think first then speak. You will have fewer regrets, if any.

* * * * *

You can save a lot of time by saying concisely what you meant.

* * * * *

A rush to judgment spoke to who you were first.

* * * * *

If you have something to say bad about a person, start with yourself first.

* * * * *

Silence is a golden opportunity to contemplate anything.

* * * * *

Kind words always have a welcoming place with any human.

* * * * *

Being at a loss for words is a brief opportunity to think. Make the best of it.

* * * * *

If a man says one thing, but does another, pay little attention to what more he says and become keen to his every move. This man likely cannot be trusted, even in the least of things.

* * * * *

If you do not have anything good to say about someone, start with yourself.

* * * * *

A wise man will keep his mouth closed to hear what he does not want to miss. He may, following much thought, act on this later. His approach is proper for unreasonable and uncontrolled challenges.

A temper is commonly accompanied by best friends regret, despair, bitterness, and unforgiving.

* * * * *

Your body language speaks to everything. It affirms or refutes what you stated, and it further speaks to what you did not state.

* * * * *

Uninvited interest in another person's affairs is your time spent not attending to your own affairs. Your unattended affairs then invite others to review your affairs. It is a contagious "merry-go-round" virus.

Choose not to go for the ride.

CHAPTER 4

A Choice of Love or Hate

When you hurt others, you must stand to be hurt back. That hurt may not necessarily come from the one you hurt but there always will be someone waiting to hurt you back for the things you know about or may not know about, because you may not realize you hurt them. Hurting then can be considered a cycle of replays, so do your part in eliminating the cycle by not hurting others yourself.

* * * * *

Always be sensitive to how others may feel about what you say before you say it. If you think it may hurt, hunker down. If it will help, start talking.

* * * * *

Love can be earned by what you do and not by what you say. Statements of "I love you" can be so overrated and misinterpreted.

* * * * *

Being calm, respectful, and gentle will normally disarm the assaults of any bully in due time. It conspicuously wears down their approach of control over you. You will soon be of no interest to them so they will move on to identify another victim to feed their bully gratifications.

* * * * *

Do not put off love, otherwise it will put you off. You get what you give.

* * * * *

Loving your enemy may not make them a better person but will surely work wonders for making you one. Your badge of excellent principles and character will be on display.

* * * * *

If being a difficult person is your brand, it will never work out for you or anyone else. Start being gentle and see all the wonderful qualities of life you have been missing.

* * * * *

Pain and suffering generally moves us to rely on someone else. Who is your source of comfort in the mist of your storms? Make sure they can help you weather it and not just present unsolicited and meaningless life instructions.

* * * * *

Live to love or at least, love to live. They are really one and the same.

* * * * *

Anger is ugly and so will be every outcome connected to it.

* * * * *

A humble demeanor peacefully quiets one's spirit and respects others to be who and how they want to be.

* * * * *

Love is powerful and can move the unmovable. That is how it works, so all you should do is love.

* * * * *

Family love is mostly a given state of relationship, but a person who loves you outside of your family does so by choice. It is likely contributable to who you are as a person.

* * * * *

Brokenness is not a desirable state, but managed reassembly can yield quantum leaps in strength, endurance, and character.

* * * * *

A move to hurt someone starts with your own self-infliction. To commit the act, you must first injure your own character and decency.

* * * * *

Oppression for the oppressed is not a choice. It is a predicament in an unspecified spell of aggression for power and authority against and over those who are perceived as being a threat or who models a scope of profitability to the oppressor's existence as they know it or wish it to be. Insistence on having oppression, ironically, shapes the oppressor into oppression by the greed of efforts to retain the desirable oppression. Oppression is always followed by a fall in status. It is a circular insanity. It is difficult to start and most difficult to eliminate. He who builds oppression knows how to get out of it, but he who becomes oppressed hardly knows where to begin the time-consuming exodus. But given that the oppressor is now subject to the oppression in the interest of retaining it, they too, are now a prisoner to their own web of oppression insanity. They will go to extremes to retain it, even to death. How sad of an outcome that the oppressor will die in oppression by their pursuit.

* * * * *

Love is a motived condition that facilitates levels of demonstrated caring.

* * * * *

The one who chooses to live without love chooses not to live. It is a prerequisite life support system that insures and promotes endurance and stability in every aspect of our lives.

* * * * *

The lowest common denominator of living is the lack of being loved or one's inability to demonstrate love.

* * * * *

The lack of love in one's life is like living with a chronic disease—sealed with a band of premature and inevitable death.

* * * * *

If anyone loves another—the one who is loved already knows; not by what was said, but what was done.

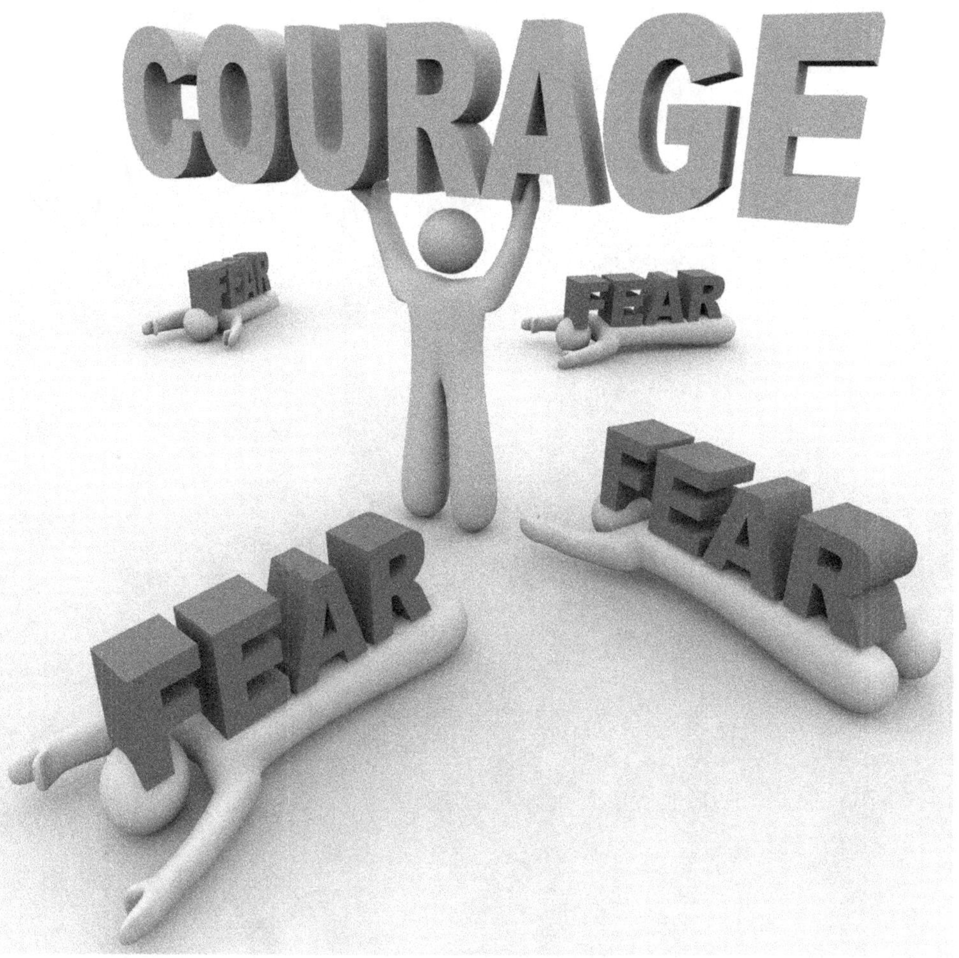
COURAGE
FEAR
FEAR
FEAR
FEAR

FEAR KILLS MORE DREAMS THAN **FAILURE** EVER WILL.

CHAPTER 5

Conquering Fear

Fear is not necessarily a bad thing. It only becomes bad when we allow it to control what we do. Fear keeps you sensitive to the presence of danger. Knowing where danger is makes all the difference in avoiding it.

* * * * *

Fear can handicap you. Your knowledge about the fear will help you safely address the unknown, which is the root of the fear.

* * * * *

Fear causes anxiety and attempts to take control over your mind and body. Fight back with two simple steps. First, educate yourself about the fear. Knowledge is power. Second, develop proactive measures to immediately address it. These actions will keep you feeling that you are in control of your fear.

* * * * *

Fear can cripple you or you can cripple fear by taking control and managing it. You may not be in control of the instance which led to the fear, but you are in control of your response to the fear and your managed response or lack thereof will make all the difference in how things turn out for you. Be in control and stay in control for your own wellness. Fear is a negative force and will always replicate the same, so it is not wise to give it a foothold to continue. Show it who's boss and take control. May the force be with you!

* * * * *

If you fear what you do not know you should get busy learning what you do not understand.

* * * * *

Courage is an intentional act of control to rise above fear.

* * * * *

Courage is fear under fire.

* * * * *

He who fears is likely wise, but he who fails to control fear will likely be subject to unwise decisions and outcomes.

PART TWO

Tips on Relating and Growing at Work

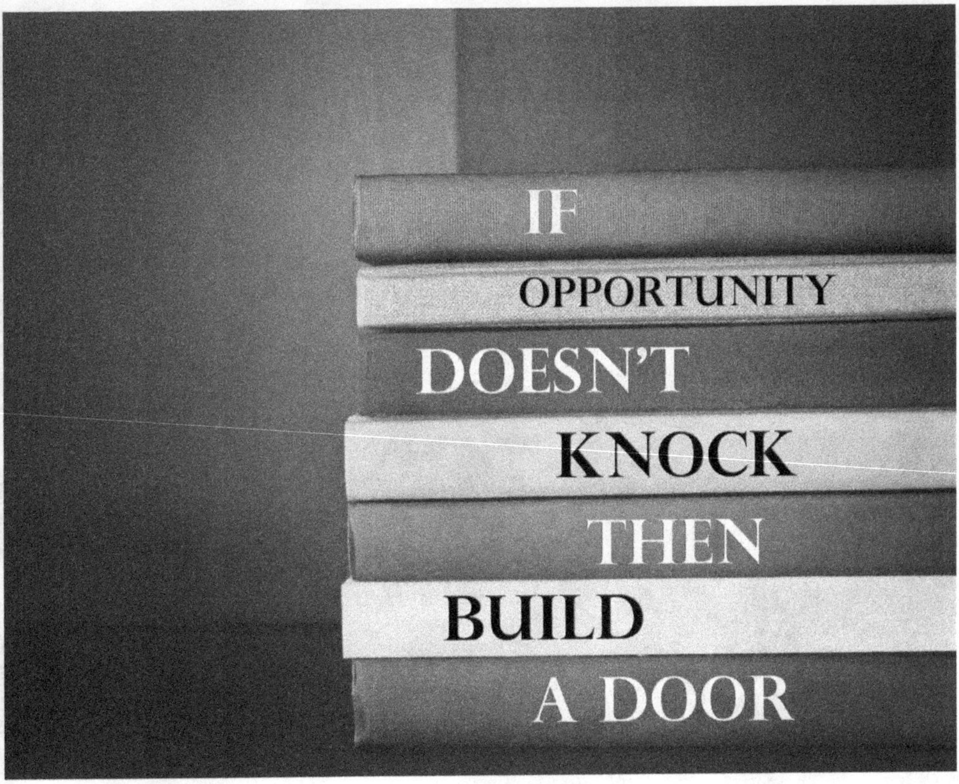
IF
OPPORTUNITY
DOESN'T
KNOCK
THEN
BUILD
A DOOR

CHAPTER 1

Tips in General

If you fear a work project you should seriously consider doing it. It could be the very project that can aggressively move you forward in your career.

* * * * *

When you go to work, *"get to work."* When you go home, *"stay there"* and leave work behind.

* * * * *

Work should never mean more than family. While it is important to the interest and welfare of all, it should never lead your focused attention. If it does, you are in the wrong job. Do not be fooled by the notion that you are working and having to disregard family for their sake. You are working against them by not spending quality time with them to grow and develop strong relationships. This cannot be compromised or put off to a later date. You will be challenged to deal with it now or later. An address later is more complex and burdensome. You will be contending with family members who have become set in their ways and use to doing things without you. Yes, you may have lost some levels of respect from family members for abandoning your family role. So, your job to do damage control later is much more difficult. The less challenging route would have been to progressively play your family role in being with them and building relationships along the way. You can build both, work and family, but they need a balance of equity planning to be sure neither one suffers or is left behind. Insist on having control and ongoing management of work-life balance.

* * * * *

Work hard and opportunities will present themselves. There will be no need for you to beg for career opportunities. They will come to you, just work hard and wait on them.

* * * * *

Work is necessary, but rest is also essential. You are always doing one or the other. Do not prolong your stay in either category.

* * * * *

Go to work meetings with an open mind for being helpful. You will be amazed at the benefit of your contributions and opportunities that will be born out of your willing engagement.

* * * * *

If you want to be noticed in life or at work, do at least one task very, very well.

* * * * *

Working hard will harden success, but hardly working will weaken the potential for success at an alarming rate.

* * * * *

Work without goals for achievement is likened to walking with your eyes closed. Who knows where or what predicament you will end up in.

* * * * *

Any time you feel your job is easy, you have outgrown it. It is time to move on and move up.

* * * * *

A career is much like surfing. You will likely fall off your board many times, but you keep getting back on and waiting for that opportunistic wave that brings fulfilling exhilaration and gratification.

* * * * *

Being in a job you do not like is likened to wearing your clothes inside out. It is odd and you would not likely do it. So, do something to move out of the job if that is your situation.

* * * * *

Everyone has a harmonious/peaceful job where the job and those you work with are in harmony with you. If you are not in that place, start looking for it.

* * * * *

If your work is not your passion, work on working your way out of it.

* * * * *

Work is relationship-building with others, while performing the same or similar task.

* * * * *

The prize of work is money, but the prize of service is spiritual and emotional gratification, which is priceless.

* * * * *

Working hard is something you should want to do and not be asked to do. It is the margin of difference between mediocre and excellence.

* * * * *

Your manager and coworkers want you to succeed.

* * * * *

No group can experience the fullness of success unless everyone in the group is successful.

* * * * *

Respect must be maintained in the workplace. No manager or employee should ever be allowed to exercise any less practice. Lack of respect by any person tears down relationships and leads to interference with the mission and bottom-line. When relationships suffer at work, so does the mission.

* * * *

Workplace misconduct must be addressed quickly, or you will otherwise risk hurting the business objectives and losing quality employees. Basically, one employee who does not comply with company policy is signaling to the employer that they really do not want to work for you and comply with your standards. So why retain them if they do not apparently like being there? The employer should kindly help them realize that fact.

* * * *

Generally, progressive discipline is a way to help an individual make up their mind about their commitment to company work and standards. A terminated employee was indecisive for too long. Do not take long in helping an individual come to terms with whether they want to comply with company standards. They either wish to do so, or they do not. Some individuals overlook that they are being paid to comply with standards. No candidate would say in an interview that things must be done by their standards and not by the company's or they would never be hired. That same logic most definitely applies after the candidate is hired because they at that point are being paid to not just work but also comply with company standards and policies as well. Unless alternatively, they were less than forthcoming in the interview or on their application about their intentions for employment. Anything short of compliance is constructive theft given that they are being paid.

* * * * *

Speaking kindly and gently to anyone in the workplace will most times return the same courtesy. It can also open all sorts of opportunities for people to speak highly of you in your absence, where and when it really counts.

* * * * *

Workplace harassment should never be tolerated. It savagely attacks work relationships and stands to kill everything in its way, including the mission.

* * * * *

Workplace bullies belong at home with themselves. They will not back down from their tactics until the employer aggressively confronts them with the consequences of their continued behavior.

* * * * *

If one employee is making everyone around them miserable you have two choices. You can take action with one employee or many employees. Be wise and logical.

* * * * *

If you find that you cannot speak well of the employer for which you work, your goal should be to work your way out of there as soon as possible.

* * * * *

If someone dislikes you at work, that is okay. Keep in mind that they are being paid to get along, but not necessarily to like you. So, their actions become nothing short of wasted emotional energy on their part.

* * * * *

A good workplace is orderly and tidy. It suggests that the employer and work divisions are the same way as well and signals confidence in the mission of the organization.

* * * * *

A good performance review is as good as the truth in it.

* * * * *

An exaggerated resume is a falsification of credentials. No person who has worked hard has any need to exaggerate what they worked on and how they did it. It is what...it is and should speak for itself.

* * * * *

Any person who gains access to a position by false pretense in skill and abilities will live in the fear of discovery and certainly, at some point, come face-to-face with having to address the misrepresentation.

* * * * *

There are many honest and careless mistakes that can be made at work, but a false official statement slays an individual's and the employer's integrity and adversely questions the very fibers of the organizations' business objectives.

* * * * *

Take no pride in telling anyone off at work. It fosters a hostile work environment.

* * * * *

Crooked people at work are likened to a crook in a rope. Once the crook is in there the only way to get it out is to pull it. So, get busy at pulling any crook out of your workplace. No successful employer advertised to have an experienced crook on staff. Crooks are all about what they can get from the company and not what they can give the company.

* * * * *

Any employee should be given chances to improve performance or conduct, but managers should be given very few chances. Any manager who needs repeated chances to improve are in the wrong job. It should be addressed before it affects the business objectives and goes beyond easy repair and damage control.

* * * * *

To move forward in your career, you must yourself put it in drive and step on it!

* * * * *

Where you are in your career is your doing by what you did or left undone.

* * * * *

A career does not just happen—you make it happen.

* * * * *

If you are upset about not moving forward in your career, it is your fault. Step around the roadblocks and move on.

* * * * *

Some people fail at making a good career because they failed to plan for one.

* * * * *

If you have no plans to succeed at what you want to do, that within itself is a plan.

* * * * *

Employers generally do not select you. You actually select them as they only respond to your application of interest.

* * * * *

You have two families: your biological and work families. Do not take either for granted. You generally interact with your work family more than you do with your biological family. Respect and value them both for what they bring to you.

* * * * *

Work should be something you enjoy doing. If you do not, you should work hard on doing something else.

* * * * *

The best thing you can do at work is to work and the next best thing is to makes serious attempts to relate well with others. You must be effective at both to be happy and successful at work.

* * * * *

Your willingness to get along with others at work is proportionate to your reasonable expectations to receive the same reaction from others.

* * * * *

Obtaining education is the art of acquiring knowledge to facilitate the engagement and application of wisdom upon occurrences which comes before us at work and in life. Applied education at work opens innumerable career opportunities. Increase your education levels to increase opportunities.

* * * * *

Make no mistake about it, honesty and trustworthiness can be discerned by your manager and coworkers. So, if you did an unfavorable act or deed, even if it could not be proven, they know by human instinct. You may have gotten away with the act, but not the ethical principle of integrity.

* * * * *

Working to just get by in your job will never stand as a promotional attribute. Your actions will be realized and qualified as such by your coworkers and management.

* * * * *

Promotion happens as a result of what you have already done and not by what you are currently doing. It is the time-consuming retrospect that is brought back into review. Make sure you are building your work history to support promotional considerations.

* * * * *

There will always be a reason for not being promoted. Find out what it is and dedicate yourself to smartly dealing with it. Productivity promotes and pouting generally does not.

* * * * *

Be serious in your considerations for promotion so that you do not subject yourself to a promotional level of incompetency by focusing on the job compensation or benefits. Being placed in a job you cannot successfully accomplish sets you up for demotion and that is a highly unfavorable career and resume marker to move past.

* * * * *

The only way to know that you are on track at work is to keep measuring the progress of your tracks.

* * * * *

A violation of ethics at work should never be anyone's secret.

* * * * *

A manager's job in career development is to make development opportunities available to employees and the employees' job is to pursue and act on those opportunities.

* * * * *

Members of senior management should never be given the permission to not *get along* with one another. It hampers the overall wellness and image of the team and puts the business objectives at risk. General managers should insist on team members being able to get along as a condition of continued employment.

* * * * *

Speaking badly about your boss in the presence of others can call into question your allegiance to your boss and the organization.

* * * * *

Attendance and punctuality are an important part of employment and speaks volumes about your allegiance and commitment to both your job and the employer's mission.

* * * * *

Wasting time at work doing things other than your job duties is nothing short of theft.

* * * * *

In these treacherous times, do not take your life for granted. Take proactive measures to help protect yourself in the event an attack occurs at your workplace. Always have a plan to escape imminent and life-threatening danger. If your employer has emergency response plans, become very acquainted with them. Knowing what to do and when to do it can save your life. You do always want to cherish being able to say, "It's just another day at work."

* * * * *

Make it a point to enjoy working. Look for ways to put innovation and excitement into your job. Think outside the box. Try new proposals on your manager about how you would like to innovate or refresh your job duties to make them more enjoyable.

* * * * *

If workplace safety is not a top priority for your employer, safely work your way out of there. Your limbs and life depend on it.

Tips for Managers and Leaders

The boss is responsible for the successful engagement of employees for a common business cause. Every boss can therefore be considered a relationship manager.

* * * * *

The best boss will be good at bringing out the best in his/her employees.

* * * * *

A difficult and unforgiving manager should be given notice to change. Their failure to do so justifies another notice to change them out of the job. The organization mission has no mention of and little room for begging managers to comply with performance expectations.

* * * * *

A manager can only be as successful as the level of competency exhibited in those who work for them. So, make wise selections.

* * * * *

Good managers help employees grow and develop beyond the point from which they first met.

* * * * *

A common thread among excellent managers is that they value their employees and have them in mind when making decisions. They include them in the decision-making process to the extent possible.

* * * * *

A good manager ensures they spend quality time with each one of their employees.

* * * * *

If you are loud and argumentative with an employee, they are likely to elevate the tone and level of challenge to make sure they are being heard. A good manager keeps calm in hopes the employee will do the same.

* * * * *

A manager acknowledges when they are wrong. It will do wonders for your credibility.

* * * * *

A manager listens closely and repeats for validation what is heard and understood.

* * * * *

If you get a new work idea from an employee, your job as a manager is to evaluate it exhaustively to see if all or any part of the idea can be implemented.

* * * * *

A manager should study each employee's skill sets and interest to see how they can best be integrated into the job. Creativity and innovation results.

* * * * *

Discover your employees. Give them an assignment with little to no instructions on how to get it done. What you get back will likely be astonishing. They will surprise you with their scope of potential.

* * * * *

On occasions, encourage your employees to write things. This art helps improve written and analytical thinking skills.

* * * * *

A good manager periodically includes something fun in one of their staff meetings. For example, a group game, relaxation exercise, funny, but tasteful YouTube clip. Morale is not about the staff agenda, but about uplifting and refreshing workplace spirits. Routine work and staff meetings will not do the trick and neither was it intended to.

* * * * *

You cannot make everyone happy at work, but everybody should at least be happy that you tried to do so.

* * * * *

A manager should always get an "A" grade in their efforts to boost employee morale. You may not always score, but you will truly win the game with your employees.

* * * * *

Effective managers do not let things happen; they make things happen.

* * * * *

A manager may in context be reserved to effectively and efficiently maintaining things at work, but a true leader will be reserved to changing things at work.

* * * * *

A great leader is actually led by his/her people.

* * * * *

Given that most workplaces are of diverse populations, organizational decisions should incorporate feedback from the diversified population. Isolated decision in a diversified workplace is a recipe for disaster and greatly weakens the mission. It fails to embrace inclusion and will ultimately lead to a failed company.

* * * * *

A key to successful management and leadership is calling on and relying on the resources available to you. Be keen on knowing what is available to you.

* * * * *

A good manager takes the time to surprise employees with a little something special on occasions. It, for example, maybe a small gift, authorized time off, allowance to leave early or come in late. They will never forget your acknowledgement of their hard work and supporting roles as employees.

* * * * *

A manager notifies an employee about undesirable performance or behavior and gives them a chance to improve. An employee is capable of change for the better, but the choice is theirs to make.

* * * * *

An effective leader influences people to do things they otherwise would not do.

* * * * *

A strong manager will not shy away from making decisions. Your decision may not always be popular, but your employees will respect you for being strong enough to make them.

* * * * *

A manager should always be mindful to project a strong image and demeanor. Employees want the confidence of knowing their manager has that quality.

* * * * *

A good manager is always ready to give an account for their course of action, whether the action has desirable or undesirable results. It signals that your course of action was not capricious, but well thought-out.

* * * * *

A strong manager/leader never lets the employee see their level of fear.

* * * * *

A good leader leaves people alone to let them do what they do best.

* * * * *

Recognizing your employees for excellent performance is a great way to increase morale and make them feel good about working for you and the organization.

* * * * *

If you handle your employees like a drill sergeant, you will move them to rely on you to get things done and your business objectives will not likely be met in your absence.

* * * * *

Leading people by fear and intimidation will confirm the leader's fear of failure and inadequacies. Managers who lead that way should not be in management. They will only replicate more of the same and continue to adversely impact the people around them and organization's mission.

* * * * *

A manager should rehearse any major presentation aloud ahead of schedule to "hear" first what they might be missing in their intended message.

* * * * *

A good manager always takes time to clearly explain any work performance task and encourages employees to ask questions about things that may not be clear for them.

* * * * *

A good manager is always approachable. Do not lean on automation as a mechanism to maintain healthy work relationships. Workplace relationships are best captured by interactive and personable presence.

* * * * *

A manager will acknowledge their mistakes and move on, but to expound upon the reason for the mistake can further bring forward other weak details about your logic.

* * * * *

A good manager takes the time to determine employee needs and stays responsively attune to the neediest.

* * * * *

A broken employee needs increased care and support and the manager is responsible for making sure they get it.

* * * * *

A strong manager can be summed up by what they do and not what they say.

* * * * *

A leader should always be the example to follow and assume you are always being observed. You then will never let your guard down to being less than the image and demeanor you wish to portray.

* * * * *

One of the fastest ways a manager can lose credibility, respect, and confidence from their employees is to show favoritism among employees. It is a damaging brand trap that is easy to fall into, but exceedingly difficult to change once the perception is in place. Stay clear of this morale and mission buster.

* * * * *

Employees will do as you say if you do what you say. Otherwise, they will say what you do. So, remember that when you are doing what you do.

CHAPTER 3

Tips for Employees

If you are frustrated with a work task or coworker, tell your manager, "I need your help with resolving this matter." They get paid in part to do that and it could be just that simple in getting a resolution.

* * * * *

Humble and respectful employees go a long way with managers and will find that their managers will be there for them when they need them most.

* * * * *

Try by some respectful measure to be known by managers in the areas for which you aspire to be employed. When job vacancies do become available, this will likely help set you apart from those who only put in an application for consideration.

* * * * *

Employees who consistently do not get along should consider going to another work group or employer. The workplace is not a boxing ring and may not be suitable for them.

* * * * *

What you say at work can and will be repeated by you or someone else. So be sure you do not mind hearing it again from another source.

* * * * *

Work is not so bad when you "get to work!"

* * * * *

Always be mindful of looking for ways to help your boss's job be a little easier.

* * * * *

An employee should work to ensure their name is not associated with gossip and personal attacks on other coworkers.

* * * * *

In the employment world of progressive discipline, a terminated employee actually terminated themselves, because they knew, that they knew, it was coming, when it came.

* * * * *

An employee will do what is right whether in the presence or absence of the manager.

* * * * *

Helping your manager succeed by the work you do for them should be one of your highest work priorities.

* * * * *

A good employee is always looking for ways to keep their "good" brand image on track.

* * * * *

Excellence and proficiency are never an accident at work. An employee should periodically monitor their established performance expectations to ensure they are being met.

* * * * *

A good employee does not have to be told to do things. They already did them.

* * * * *

The best employee puts their best into any task at hand.

* * * * *

An employee should work hard to improve upon a task they are not good at. You can afford to do that, because the task you are good at you hardly need to work at getting it done. The time to improve is therefore on your side.

* * * * *

A good employee will always be willing to help a coworker struggling with a work task when time allows.

* * * * *

Managers are human too and not always capable of making every good and perfect decision. They are growing in their roles as well, so do not be too hard on them.

* * * * *

A good employee works hard at being and staying that way—good.

PART THREE

Thoughts on Growing Spiritually— Poetically Speaking

The Knowledge of Wisdom

Knowledge is understanding matters.
Wisdom is knowing which matters,
really matter.

Pair in the Air

I long Jesus Christ to see your face
In the white clouds a heavenly place

No man lives among the hills I see
But the power of God is revealed to me

Release my soul from pain and despair
Looking to the moment when I am caught up in the air

Content with where I am in each and every case
With Christ being near it is a very special place

Everywhere I go God also will be
Helping with my crosses and looking out for me

Walking away from God I do not dare
Waiting for the moment when I am caught up in the air

Looking and waiting until I am caught up in the air
Because my name was in the book to be in Jesus's care

Sick in the Stomach

I am impounded in my dilemma.
O Jonah, how I know what you felt.
What, Lord, has been my lack of compliance?
My neglect is ever before me.
The entrapment torments me continuously.
The best discipline is dilemma.
O God, thank you for my dilemma—to compliance.

Riding Out the Storm

My life became a storm one day. I rained tears that formed like rivers; they overflowed their banks. My emotions were like the wind, changing vectors constantly. My life was being channeled by indecisive and reckless persuasion.

The reality of the storm flashed inside of me like lightening, painfully massaging despair and the vulnerability of my heart.

My peace and stability were greatly threatened and were merging into a format of erosion. I was transformed into a model of nonconformity; far removed from the definition of average.

It appeared that my soul was being washed down a dissipating stream to an incompatible resting place—one hostile to my existence. I was weathered into a state of numbness; something outside of the realms of reality.

I became a relative of the obscure.

My closest of kin were emptiness, loneliness, and a lack of self-worth.

The storm was treacherous, and its savagery claimed victory over me.

I was wet and beaten into what I perceived as being the point of no return.

I, in my own way, sought refuge from my
holes of inadequacy.

None though, no—not one, was sufficient in offering resolution or reconciliation.

I called on the Lord.

To my surprise and lack of understanding, he told me that he never intended for me to go through that storm. He told me that his forecast had a little overcast, but was followed by clear blue skies and sunshine.

He told me that I should have asked him to manage my weather.

I allowed him to take charge immediately. My weather then aligned itself into a fashionable oasis of the tropics.

When the sun shined, it was beautiful...

When the rain came, it was beautiful... Ask Jesus... Come into a residence of peace...

Come in...out of the storm.

Hostile Pit

I am in this alone it appears.
No allies about, it brings me to tears.
I stand my ground, but rarely win.
But I have my dignity, and my closest of kin.
I do not fit in and no one seems to really care.
I will just try and mind my own business and stay in my chair.
Now I know how the ugly duckling felt.
Some days passed, I thought I would melt.
But the good Lord was with me in all these matters.
But I always felt I was amidst upset rattlers.
God was on my side and I made it out alive.
He gave me an agent to put the vipers aside.
Now I have nothing but rainbow—blue skies.
Thank you, Lord, for putting out my uncontrollable fires.

Majestic Postcards

Blue skies and rich plains
Deep valleys just the same
Show God's beauty rich and plenty
Cost you noting not even a penny
Big-big mountains snow caps too
Breathtaking photography done just for you

Troubling Waters

I was concerned when my sea became upset.
The waves became walls of entrapment.
For the moment—I saw it that way.
The chemistry of the tides emitted a scent of certain death
to whomever it touched.
Its fury was unforgiving. I had no ventilation or refuge.
I was a hostage; not to that of hospitality, but to violence and
destruction.
The ferocious waves continuously outlined
a clear definition of death.
The encampment was greater than I.
Oh Lord, what shall come of me—shall I die?
Then, I called out to the Lord… My Lord, help me!
He heard me and said, "Peace—be still."
The chaos ceased and my life became
anchored again.

God's Empowerment

I have eyes, yet I am blind.
I have ears, yet I am deaf.
I have limbs, yet I am immobile.
I have fear; known and unknown.
I have troubles, they torment me daily.
I have sin, it feeds on these trends.
Now I have God—the end of trendy sin.

They Told Me I Could Not

They said that I would not be able
to climb that mountain.
They told me it was too steep and that I would not make it to
the top,
no less the other side.
They said I would die in my attempt.
They told me that I would not be
successful just because I was—who I was.
They did not know who I knew, who my helper was,
or who was on my side.
I started my journey and made it about a third
of the way up the side of the mountain. I stopped,
turned back, came down, and turned about.
I looked up at the awesome elevation of the
mountain and said,
in the name of Jesus Christ—move!
There before me, I then saw—what had been a mountain,
was now a wet mole hill.
I stepped on it!
There are different ways of becoming successful.
In this matter, I was made to succeed.
I will claim this victory recipe to conquer
every other mountain put before me.

Taking a Stand

My eyes can see,
but not far enough.
My ears can hear,
but not all to be heard.
My feet are balanced,
but I stand to fall.
My heart is steady,
in Christ I call.
In Christ I confess,
I am standing tall.

Wondering When

I wonder o Lord, when you will come for me.
I wonder o Lord, when I get to see.
I wonder o Lord, when you will come for me.
I wonder o Lord, when I will get to be.

I wonder o Lord, when you will come for me.
I wonder o Lord, when I will use the key.
I wonder o Lord, when you will come for me.
I wonder o Lord, when heaven I will see.

A Mountain

There was a mountain in my way.
There it was with all its might.
Looking down on me with disregard.
His feet were bigger than me.
Should he move,
I shall surely be crushed.
He showed his strength by carrying many lives,
so big—they called him home.
Though I am small to him,
I know his Maker, but
he has no mind of that.
He has changed since being made.
Because our Maker is in me and not him,
I commanded him to move, in the name of Jesus Christ,
and so, it was.
In Christ, I have crushed
another insurmountable mountain.

Understanding Now

I can see the sky
But there is black in my eye
I can hear them talking
But I would rather be walking
I can feel the caring
But I am cool to the pairing
I can feel it's right
I will have my sight
I cannot walk away from this—no, no, no.
It is God calling on my inner core.

Deception of Relationship

Always on the patrol to take away the vows
Not before the act to meet gratification
Progressively dismantling the heart's fiber with its plows
Not consciously making obvious the new classification

Oh, move away from the one you seek
Less they stumble and submit to the web trap
Move away from the heart's vulnerability so bleak
Lose the hold on them for the new defining map

Missing Out

I can see what I've been missing
Lurking inside education's door

I can see what I've been missing
Shuffling across the dance room floor

I can see what I've been missing
By observation of others with so much more

I can see what I've been missing
On the boat's study ore

Share with me what I've been missing
A life of luxury what I've been missing

Let my lips taste in kissing
A life in abundance, what I've been missing

A
Journey
of a
THOUSAND
MILES
BEGINS WITH A
SINGLE
STEP

The Struggle

My instincts charged forward—my essence called out.
For some reason I needed purpose.
I needed,
and I needed others to need me
by whatever context,
the range of needs were there.

I embarked on this needy journey.
Many though, did not want me to succeed.
They had their reasons, but I had no mind of that.
My goal was to be what the others needed me to be.

They told me that I would need to come from where I was to be who I
wanted to be.
I had to leave the valley.
So,

I pulled myself up from the bottom of the valley.
When I arrived at the top,
They said—welcome to the bottom of the mountain,
but what you are looking for is at the top of the mountain.
So,

I pulled myself up from the bottom of the mountain.
They then said—welcome to the top of the mountain,
but what you are looking for lies at the bottom of the valley.
Those that need you.
Their manner and address revealed their dislike with my
presence.

They said—you must return to those who need you
I said, after careful thought, no thank you.
I will stay here at the top
as a symbol to those who wish to follow.
To those who have the same hunger as I did.
My arrival represents accomplishment.
That is the need of the people in the valley.
A sense of accomplishment.
Coming up from the bottom in any measure,
is noteworthy achievement.
Many may try and fail,
but I still want to represent the incentive.
No thank you again,
I choose to be the benchmark of this struggle.
Furthermore, you are still here
and it must therefore have some profitability.
I will wait on the others right here.
They will come.
I know they will come.
Their instincts will call them forward.

Leaving My Mark

When death has taken me from this place,
tell them who I was.
When the sound of my voice is no more,
tell them what I did.
When my restitution has come forward,
tell them who and what I represented.

Oh Lord, let them say I tried to be like You.
Oh Lord, let them say I hallmarked in Christ.

Tell them... I tried
to encourage others to be like Christ,
even when it was not stated.

Tell them, how I loved them—
though the lily of the valley of peace
sealed my lips before I could tell them...
Tell them.

I want to leave a mark for Christ.
I want to be remembered in the service of
the will of God; not a self-centered agenda of man.

Tell them... Tell them I was a policeman—
Policing relief for the broken hearted.

Tell them I was a fireman—
Putting out burning anger and hostility. Tell them.

Tell them I tried to be a band leader for
peace, righteousness, and happiness.

Tell them I was a pharmacist—
Medicating minds and hearts with the hope
and promise of Jesus Christ. Tell them.

Tell them I attempted by every chance, to be the
president of tolerance, reconciliation, peace, and equality.

Tell them I tried to be an engineer
of positive motivation, an architect of new
defined beginnings—tell them.

Tell them I was an advocate for the
gift of another citizenship…tell them.

Tell them though, from all my attempts, I was yet weak. I missed my
mark by what more I could have done. I was so distant from what
Christ was, but I desired to live up to what he wanted me to be.
Giving my love, peace and joy to others.

Tell them, I will wish to see them there in heaven.
I hope my mark moved some heart and soul to see
me there…tell them.

But here now, tell them to look up, and be of good cheer for me.
I am with the King.
I knew to be confident of that very thing according to his good
promise.

I hope to see you in the white clouds—our meeting
place. Long my friend to see his face, in the white clouds our meeting
place.

No man lives among the hills you will see, but in his presence we will surely be.

May the Spirit of God's peace be with you now and eternally.

Wondering Wind

I did not see the wind, but I saw its effects.
Blowing trees, limbs, paper, hair, and things.
Nothing exposed can have refuge. Its choice
of direction affects anyone, or anything in its path.
It is like the unseen spirits; good and bad.
They cannot be seen, but can affect what is subject to them.
You however, by choice, may repel good or bad...
To repel one is to accept the other...

Big Man, Little Man

What great man shall boast about his works
When the Lord was the one who gave him his perks

What great man shall say look what I did
When the Lord touched his life from when he was a kid

What great man will boast of what he has
When the Lord blessed him all through his past

What great man can brag on what he said
When the Lord designed the very brain in his head

What small man shall not boast but give God thanks
A great big man investing in heaven's big bank

Looking for Success

I looked back and saw where I came from.
I looked forward and saw where I was going.
I looked down and saw where I was.

All that looking; no action.
One can become absorbed with
observation and analysis.

While you are on the information highway,
don't get run over by becoming addicted to looking and search.

Pricing Anything Good

We consistently chose not to have it in our lives.
We consistently avoid the associated attachments
to free ourselves.

We often fail to speak or act
because it will hold us captive from the onset.
It is a painful episode of commitment
that produces discipline and respect,
but we often do not care to experience it.

To have a quality life one must be subject to it,
and to reject it is to take the "quality" out of life.
Growth and development are contingent on it,
in every aspect of our lives.

It brings forward independence and reliability in us all.

It is *accountability* my friend—*accountability*!

Being Happy

I saw the sunshine and I was happy.
I saw the snow and I was happy.
I saw the rain and I became sad.
I saw the storm and
I then knew when to be glad.

Fill Up

We are truly fulfilled
by
fulfilling others.

I Can Know

I can see, but I cannot really see anything.
I can feel, but I really do not feel anything.
I can hear, but I did not really hear anything.
When I am in fellowship with the Holy Spirit,
I can see, feel, and hear things that I otherwise could not.
Thank you, God.

Seasonal People

People are like the seasons
they change—We know however
in which order the seasons come,
but with people, we sometimes hardly know
what season to expect.

Waiting

I am trying my best to wait on the Lord, but my heart
flutters at the notion of entertaining my circumstances.

And if I move to construct my future,
will it not be laced with the destruction of my blindness?

God surely holds my life's panoramic vision of perfection,
a comparatively awesome review
from that of my own insignificant anchor of fate.

What can I do that will be greater than he that is within me?
I am embarrassed by my contemplation
and it emerged with my conduct of disregard.

Who or what has stolen my remembrance of his promises?
Rebuke it, Lord, so that I might get my pillows of priorities
straight again.

How can it be, that I will ignore with impatience
the throne of Grace and Glory; dripping exceedingly
with the abundance of infinite love and mercy?

Order my steps o Magnificent Lord of the universe.
How am I worthy of such independent and personal attention?
Thanks, and glory be to God that he was, is, and always will be
our God of hope, promise, and deliverance in all things.

Hallelujah—Amen.

Understanding

Run, but not fast.
Walk, but not slow.
Talk, but not quickly.
Understand all to be understood.

Alone

I am alone,
but I am not lonely.

I love being alone,
the earth is my company.

Oh, how I learn about me

when I am alone.

I am my own company and friend too.

The King

The King of kings—Jesus Christ

Grace

Playing my role to secure my soul.
Nothing I do will make it unfold.

But by his grace, he claims my soul.
Dwells in me—with his precious golds.

Lifting me up with other winning souls.
Confirming my place and heavenly goal.

I Want

I want to know
the color of good

I want to know
the weight of generosity

I want to know
the taste of prosperity

I want to know
the feel of hope

I want to know
the sound of promise

I want to know
the smell of victory

He paid my price
I know all things (I need to know) through Christ

Visitations

He visits me sometimes without announcement.
He reaffirms his dwelling place sometimes without prior notice.
Sometimes when I least expect it, he massages my heart and mind.
He will not let me forget he is there and who I belong to.
Oh, Holy Spirit,
how I love you so.

Where?

God is always there for you—
There where you are—
No matter what—
He is always there—
Always!

Any feelings that he is not there will never stand to prove or qualify his absence. He is there with you now so go ahead and *smile.*

Now

I cry out and he hears me...
He responds in perfected timing.

Unconditional Love

That love defined by the boundaries of the sky.
The love that flows like the open flood gates
of the greatest dam.
Sometimes difficult to defend—
Sometimes difficult to justify—
Always difficult to hold back—

Controls

I looked asunder
I moved like the wind
I controlled my destiny like the snow does the ground
Thank God I am not in control anymore
And allowed him to take control
Now I am a
Vector of success

Bad Things

How is this, Lord, that you have allowed these bad things to happen?
How is it, Lord, that I have failed to thank you for all
the other bad things that did not happen,
because you circumvented them before they happened.
How is it, Lord, that I think you could have missed anything?
It happened either by your intent or allowance and it must then have
divine purpose behind it.
I will trust you either way…keeping confident
that you are not missing anything and it will all work for good.
Thank you, God.

Searching for Perfection

Perfection?
Look no further—

The Messiah—Jesus Christ is

your answer.

Excuse Me, Lord

Excuse me, Lord, for being self-centered.
I have failed you terribly.
I have played games with you by rationalizing my permit
to sin, but you were watching me. And who Lord will be worthy of
casting the first stone against me?
I have ignored you much of my time.
I lived by assumption—because I did not need you to
breathe.
It was something that just happened.
I have spoken with disregard—as if you had nothing
to do with my life.
I have wrongfully boasted my accomplishments,
as if I single-handedly did it all.
O Lord my God, forgive me for my sins.
May your mercy and grace be with me forever.

Thank You, Lord

Thank you, Lord,
...That you did not order your wrath against me
when I walked with a self-centered agenda.

...For your grace,
when I chose to give my allegiance to a sinful campaign.
In opposition to your will.

...For your patience and kindness,
when I deliberately rebelled against you
to suit my own gratifications.

Thanks, and glory be to God that you restrained your wrath
and generated grace and patience with me.
Thank you, Lord.

Thanksgiving to the Almighty God

Thanksgiving
...For his mercy,
regarding those unrighteous things that I've done and
the righteous things I left undone.

...For his grace,
following my sin; that I am still alive.

...For his compassion,
regarding the things I do that are most displeasing before him.

...For his continuous love,
when I did not act as if I loved him.

About-Face

I have strayed from you, o Lord.
For I know from deep in my soul that you are worthy of my surrender
to service.

I have failed you, Lord, in every possible way. I have fallen
short of your expectations.

By my own acknowledgement of transgressions, I conclude that I must
be driven by foolish ambitions.

I recognize in my heart and spirit that you are my Savior
and the Redeemer of my soul.

O God Almighty, forgive me for my sins. Have mercy
on me in my misguided and foolish ways.

May your forgiveness, loving kindness, and grace, be with me as I go.

I am so deeply indebted to you, yet my repayment is so little.

You have repeatedly furnished me with undeserving
grace and mercy.
God, restore my soul to your glorious riches in the willingness to do
your will.
O my God, I ask of thee, Most High and Awesome God,
forgive me my sins—more times than I can ask.
I understand your role and my place.
I seek thee.
I want to be prepared at all times for your day of deliverance.

I Thank You, Father God

I thank you for the blessings you have given me
…those that I can see
…those that I cannot see
(those you did anyway because you loved me)

…those that I can understand
…those that I cannot understand
(within my human mind)

…those that are known to me
…those that are known to me
(because in your mercy, you choose to take care of them for me)

Mercy and Grace

O Lord my God
my Most High and Sovereign God,
I have continuously fallen short of your glory.

My iniquities are ever before me.

I masquerade my sin before men,
but how can I hide my violations from your face?

I seem to justify my transgressions
by accounting for times that I have been transgressed,
but that is not right.

Embarrassed by my acknowledgement,
I have even moved to blame you
for not being there in my time of need…but
of course,
you were always there.

Thank you for being patient with me
while I attempt to get my attitude and
your business with me
on track.

I sincerely thank you, Lord,
for the mercies and grace
you have given me.

Thank you, Lord.

Thank You—God the Father

Thank you for being you.

The great and Omnipotent God
Father and Creator of all things for good cause.
Many things for which I am not able to understand.

Thank you, Almighty Most High Supreme God of the universe.

Thank you for your wonderful love of reconciliation by
sending your Son and our Savior Jesus Christ to die for the sins
of this world.

Thank you for sending God—the Holy Spirit, another essence of who
you are to those who would believe in the life, death and resurrection
of your Son Jesus Christ.

Thank you from the bottom of my heart, as many times as can be said.
May my spirit repeat that sound in joy.

Thank you, Father—thank you.

O Jesus

O Jesus, my sight to see,
who shines his light for me to see.

O Jesus, my rock, my horn, the strength for me.
In your presence I long to be.

O Lord, my Jesus it is good for me.
Your blessing following from the deity.

O my Jesus, I am pleased as I can be,
O my Jesus, you have really blessed me.

O Jesus! Thanks for the peace and deliverance.

The face of your presence I wait to see.

Hopeful Blessings

May the mercy and goodness of God be with you.

May his blessings of promise and
salvation show you what to do.

May there be no incidents of misfortune
which cause you to be blue.

May God's sweet presence be with you
all the day through.

Jesus Was the Man

Jesus was the Man,
who brought forward the Father's master plan.

He died on the cross and paid our cost
and now I am found but once was lost.

Spilled his blood for me you see,
so, in heaven with the Father, I will get to be.

Touched by the Spirit, he made me whole,
and now I feel like solid gold.

Touched by the Spirit, can you feel him move,
and I got a new Teacher and a brand-new school.

Glory be to God, for his mercy and grace,
he gave us Jesus, who is preparing our place.

I cannot wait to see him in the white clouds,
I cannot wait to see him, I will be so proud.

Jesus is my companion and a real good friend,
because he sticks with me through thick and thin.

Glory be to God that he gave his only Son,
that my soul is spared and in hell will not burn.

Blessed in the Lord who came to me,
he gave me sight, and now I see.

Do you have trouble and are full of despair?
Turn to Jesus, he'll fix your affair.

Feel God's Spirit while I sing this song,
let him in your heart, to make a spiritual bond.

Thanks be to God, I am not the same,
he provided for my rest when Jesus came.

Don't you hear Jesus, don't you hear him call?
Please reach out to him, before you go and fall.

Jesus is the man, King and divine,
give him your life, while you still have time.

The Savior Jesus

I asked him one day to be mine
and he said yes. Embraced me lovingly as one of his very own.
How wonderfully privileged to be claimed by him,
and to anyone else who ask for the free gift.
Salvation—the most incomparable and comprehensive gift of love.

Exposed

Your exposure to good things will likely promote the continuation of such things.

Your exposure to bad things is likely to promote the continuation of such things.

Exposure is then relative and predictable. Your exposure status is normally directly proportionate to the active state of its embodiment.

Existence in one will choke off opportunity for the other.

Understanding What

If you can see and understand anything better than others,
you are not better—
you are blessed.

Prayer

Pray and have the Creator of the
universe pay special attention to you.

Pray when you think it is working.
Pray when you do not think it is working.
Pray until something is working.

Go to God in sincere prayer and he
will hear your first and last words.

He will act on your prayer when he
knows it is just the perfect time for you.

God's Answer

God's lack of response to
doing what you want him
to do
is within itself—

an answer.

Forever Minds
(The Tip That Really Matters)

God has created all things. His creation of man was done with forever in mind.

You will live forever. Where you live will be your choice. Through Jesus Christ, we are given a gift and chance to have eternal comfort and to live our lives in heaven eternally with our Father, the Creator.

On the other hand, you may choose not to accept Christ and subject yourself to living in hell—eternally. An existence of continuous torment that lacks peace and comfort and that experience will never end and can never be changed. Surely, that is not what you are enthusiastically looking forward to in your eternal existence.

Where will you live heaven or hell? Do you really choose eternal torment in hell? Your actions or lack thereof, may be answering the question for you. Are you a heaven or hell shareholder? Are your actions buying stock for heaven or hell?

If you have not already asked Jesus to forgive your sins and come into your life as your personal Savior, ask now and your sincere request will invest you for heaven immediately. Take action and trust him to do the right good thing for you. Do not wonder if it will work for you, because it will work for you as soon as you finish asking him to be your Savior. It is that simple.

You do not need to understand everything, you just need to understand that you need to rely on a stronger source than yourself and from what you are being told that Source is Jesus and he can guarantee you an abundant and quality life now and beyond the life we know here on Earth today. Just try him with this simple prayer.

Tell Jesus you are being told that you are broken in what he defines as sin. That you would like him to forgive your sins and to save you for eternal life with him in heaven by becoming your personal Savior. In Jesus name. Amen.

He will immediately respond to your sincere request and accept and save you as being one of his own children. Of all the things that matter in life, this is the *one* that *matters* the *most*. If you prayed that simple prayer, you are now a child of God. Get in a Bible-based church and grow in the delight of his presence with you.

Report

When the accountability of your life is before God in judgment, how much time will it show you did in service to his work?

Hours? Days? Weeks? Months? Years?

You will see and account for your life again down to the second. Will you be embarrassed by your service record or stand tall by having pleased the Lord in your service? Will God find favor or fault in your actions? Will he say that you spent much of your time praising Him, being Christ-like, and following his will for your life? Will you pass the accountability tests? If you do not know, you need to run a Christian checklist on your actions and take corrective action where necessary.

Private Moments

If you knew someone (angel or demon) was observing you where you are this very moment, would you still keep doing what you are doing? Your actions will serve to rebuke one and invite the other in to assist with the continuation of what it is you are doing. Well guess what? It is highly probable that you are being watched this very moment. What are you are doing? Keep this notion in mind wherever you go and with everything you do. I hope this moves you forward to secure or reaffirm your salvation or commitment in Christ.

Staging for the Worst

Brace yourself against the worst odds by depending on Jesus Christ to see you through everything. The loss of a loved one, job, marriage, money, emotional stability, and any other devastating occurrences. Know that on the other end of any predicament is Jesus Christ. He will get to the other end the same way you did—by going through it with you. Just remember that the matter had a beginning and it also has an ending. God is the Alpha and Omega and while he may not have had much to do with the beginning of the situation, it is reassuring to know he has authority over the end. He will be at the beginning of all things and at the end. He is always the hope that all is not lost.

Ready, Set, Go

If you know the beginning and end of some occurrence (good or bad), why would you not do what it takes to be part of the good ending. Read Genesis and Revelation; the first and last books of the Bible. Oh yes, read the other books to see how the beginning makes it to the end. Which ending will you chose to be part of—the good or bad? Seek the Savior Jesus Christ with the authoritative good ending.

Love Forevermore

I love to press on your lips
alongside our glasses to sip

I long to hold you near and close
Awakening my emotions so I can boast

I think of you in hostage thought
A gentle message of my soul it brought

I contemplate our shared moments in time
A wonder of beauty in your presence I find

Give me your hand in a relationship trip
Before the influence overcome us from the glasses we sip

Being together is the dream I dare
Make me happy to avoid pity in despair

Confirm your heart's awaking and make us a pair
A bond to stand and support this awesome affair

Presence

I want to always see you and when I do
I become a nervous wreck and do not know what to do.

I try and capture my breathe
but somehow, I become deflated in your presence
and words are no more than a few.

I want to always touch you, but my fear restricts my dare to do so.

But oh, how I wish I could wrap my arms around you
so that you would without doubt
know what I feel for you is as deep as an ocean floor.

If I only knew how to access the love in your door.

Divine Diversity

God created all things including the "peoples."

God is a God of diversity given that he chose to make many of us different in so many ways. Diversity in race, gender, and abilities are what we realize most.

If you believe in God, you must believe in diversity—accepting, loving, and caring for those different from you...they too are his creations.

The Wave of Jesus

Catch the wave of Jesus Christ…the wave of peace and excellence for eternal life. Confessing your sins, asking for forgiveness and for Jesus to be your Savior for an eternity is the best wave you can catch.

Surf's up!

Living Without Jesus Christ Is Like

Taking off on a jet and realizing after takeoff that your landing gear has just dropped off.

Going on a boat ride in unexpected choppy waters when you realize your patches and motion sickness pills are in your other pants' pocket.

Going for sky diving lessons and just after you have jumped from the plane, you discover that you only have the "para" part of the "chute" because the chute has a gaping hole in it.

Getting all your shopping done and glad you did, only to find your cash and credit cards are in your other wallet.

Taking a forty-mile motor bike ride through the desert and after twenty miles into the adventure, you note that the vehicle before you lost a bag load of sharp-edge nails on the roadway.

Watching the gorillas at the zoo when the zoo attendant accidentally bumped his service cart into the fence, snapping the protective barrier between you and them.

Getting three feet into your bungee jump and your peripheral vision detects that the end of the cord had not been properly secured to the bridge.

Realizing you have just taken a hard fall from a five hundred-pound bull, only to find your bearings to realize you're eye-to-eye.

While you are crossing a small everglades channel bridge infested with alligators, you note the bridge's support structure starts to give way.

Visiting Yellowstone and getting that close-up of the bears and happy that you were able to do so, quickly return to your car as the bears approach, only to realize that you locked your keys in the car.

choose

- TO BE -

happy

ABOUT THE AUTHOR

Dr. Wilbur Hill is originally from Mississippi and currently lives in Florida. He served as an officer in the United States Air Force. His career comprises extensive human resources experience. He recently retired as the vice president of Human Resources for an electric company. Wilbur has a passion for motivating and inspiring people. He has a doctorate in Biblical Counseling.

CPSIA information can be obtained
at www.ICGtesting.com
Printed in the USA
FSHW011948130221
78568FS